Great Autumn Food Made Simple

John Topham

LAMONA & John Topham

The Perfect Combination

John Topham

Great Autumn Food Made Simple

As the nights draw in and the temperature drops, our cooking and eating habits change. We want comforting, reassuring food that keeps out the cold – and we're happy to spend time in a cosy kitchen preparing it. Stews, soups, roasts and hot puddings are firm favourites on the menu, for family meals and entertaining. I've included plenty of these here, all making use of the amazing seasonal ingredients we get in Britain at this time of year.

This book also features recipes for autumn's two big celebrations: Bonfire Night and Halloween. I hope you'll enjoy making your own traditional treats, such as gingerbread, toffee apples and toasted marshmallows. The kids will love them – if the adults don't get there first!

All these recipes are tried and tested on Lamona appliances, so you can be confident they'll turn out well. Even if you cook only occasionally, you'll find my step-by-step instructions easy to follow – and the results well worth the small amount of effort. Or if you've an experienced cook looking for new ideas, there's lots of inspiration here for you too.

For all types of cook, in all shapes and sizes of kitchen, Lamona appliances give you all the choice you need. With their help, you'll soon be cooking up the very best of autumn.

John Topham

Head Chef and owner, The General Tarleton

LAMONA & John Topham
The Perfect Combination

The General Tarleton

Soups

08 Roast Spiced Squash Soup with a Garden
   Sage Cream
10 Classic French Onion Soup
12 Chickpea, Lamb and Coriander Soup
14 Fish Soup with Gruyère, Croutons and Rouille
18 Celeriac and Smoked Bacon Soup

Slow Cooked Recipes

22 Slow Cooking
24 Steak and Ale Pudding
26 Hungarian Goulash
28 Beef Stew and Dumplings
30 Honey Roast Ham Hocks and Baked Beans
32 Braised Short Rib of Beef with a Red
   Wine Reduction
36 Coq au Vin
38 Lancashire Hotpot
40 Butternut Squash Filled with Roast Roots,
   Plum Purée and Celeriac Cream
44 Lamb and Apricot Tagine
46 Creamed Rice Pudding and Autumn Fruits
48 Bread and Butter Pudding

Autumn Classics

52 Smoked Haddock and Welsh Rarebit
54 Roast Loin of Pork with Cinnamon and Apple
56 Pan Roast Rack of Venison with Chocolate Sauce
60 Roast Partridge with Pancetta and Braised Cabbage
62 Warm Roast Pigeon with Beetroot Salad
64 Coquilles St Jacques
66 Pumpkin Risotto
68 Seafood Thermidor
70 Roast Butternut Wedges with Hazelnuts, Goats'
   Cheese and Pesto
72 Melting Chocolate Fondant
74 Apple Pie
78 Slow Roast Spiced Plums and Vanilla Panna Cotta

Seasonal Sides

84 Cauliflower Cheese
86 Thrice Cooked Chips
88 Roast Autumn Roots, Sage and Maple Glaze
90 Silky Mashed Potatoes

Bonfire and Halloween

94 Pumpkin Tart
98 Gingerbread
100 Bonfire Toffee
102 Toffee Apples
104 Toasted Homemade Marshmallows
106 Damson Gin
108 Hot Chocolate

110 Lamona Appliance, Sink and Tap Collection
112 The General Tarleton

Soups

Hearty, satisfying and, of course, very warming, each of these soups can be a meal in itself. Or you can make them the start to a family supper or dinner party – the interesting combinations of tastes and textures will impress even the hungriest guests.

Roast Spiced Squash Soup with a Garden Sage Cream

The slight sweetness of butternut squash really lends itself to the gentle heat of chilli and paprika – and the crème fraîche adds a touch of lightness to this hearty soup.

Serves 6 15 mins preparation, 50 mins cooking

Ingredients

1 butternut squash, peeled and diced
1 sweet potato, peeled and diced
50g unsalted butter
¼ teaspoon dried chilli flakes
½ teaspoon paprika
20 fresh sage leaves
Sea salt and milled black pepper
1 onion, peeled and diced
2 cloves garlic, peeled and sliced

1 litre vegetable stock
1 tablespoon olive oil
2 tablespoons crème fraîche

Roasting tin
Food processor

1. Pre-heat the oven to 180°C/gas mark 4.

2. Place the squash and sweet potato in a roasting tin. Scatter with 30g of the butter, and sprinkle with the chilli flakes, paprika and half of the sage leaves. Season with salt and pepper, cover with tin foil and roast in the oven for 30 minutes.

3. Meanwhile, heat a large, heavy-bottomed pan, and add the remaining butter. When this is foaming, add the onion and garlic, and cook for 5 minutes, stirring until they are soft but not turning brown.

4. Remove the squash and sweet potato from the oven and pour over the onions. Add the vegetable stock and bring to the boil. Reduce the heat and simmer for 10 minutes.

5. Remove the soup from the heat and blend in a food processor or liquidiser until smooth. Return it to a clean pan and bring back to a simmer. Check the seasoning, adding salt and pepper if necessary.

6. Heat a small frying pan until it's smoking. Add the olive oil and fry the remaining sage leaves until they are crisp but not brown. Carefully place them on some kitchen paper and sprinkle with a little salt.

7. To serve, pour the soup into bowls, drizzle with the crème fraîche and finish with a scatter of sage leaves.

Roast Spiced Squash Soup with a Garden Sage Cream

Classic French Onion Soup

Classic French Onion Soup

If you need warming up on a chilly day, there's nothing better than this timeless dish. Rich and luxurious – yet all from simple ingredients – it makes a satisfying lunch or supper.

Serves 4 30 mins preparation, 1 hour cooking

Ingredients
3 tablespoons vegetable oil
30g unsalted butter
5 onions, peeled and thinly sliced
4 cloves garlic, peeled and finely chopped
2 sprigs fresh thyme
Sea salt and milled black pepper
250ml red wine
1 litre beef stock
4 tablespoons olive oil
8 thin slices French bread
120g Gruyère cheese, grated

1. Heat the vegetable oil and butter in a heavy-bottomed pan, add the onions and cook over a medium heat for 10 minutes, stirring frequently.

2. Add the garlic and thyme, and season with a little salt and pepper. Cover with a lid and cook gently for 15-20 minutes, stirring occasionally.

3. Increase the heat, add the wine and boil until the wine has evaporated.

4. Pour in the stock and bring back to the boil, skim off any fat or sediment with a ladle and simmer gently for 30 minutes.

5. Heat a large frying pan, add the olive oil and fry the French bread slices until crisp and golden on both sides. Drain on kitchen paper.

6. Turn the grill onto to the highest setting. Ladle the soup into 4 deep-sided bowls, place 2 French bread slices on top of each and cover with Gruyère cheese.

7. Place under the grill, cook until golden and serve.

Chickpea, Lamb and Coriander Soup

Chickpea, Lamb and Coriander Soup

Serves 4-6 50 mins preparation, 2 hours cooking

Ingredients

4 tablespoons olive oil
2 onions, peeled and finely chopped
4 cloves garlic, peeled and finely chopped
500g shoulder of lamb, trimmed of excess fat and cut into small pieces
2 teaspoons paprika
2 teaspoons ground cumin
3 ground cloves
1 bay leaf
2 tablespoons tomato purée
1 litre beef stock
2 x 300g tinned chickpeas, rinsed and drained
600g tinned chopped tomatoes

2 red peppers, deseeded and cut into quarters
Sea salt and milled black pepper

To serve

1 bunch fresh coriander, chopped (plus extra leaves for garnish)
12 black olives

Roasting tray

1. Pre-heat the oven to 200°C/gas mark 6.

2. Heat 2 tablespoons of the olive oil in a large, heavy-bottomed pan. Add the onions and garlic, and cook for 5 minutes until softened. Remove from the pan and reserve.

3. In the same pan, seal and brown the lamb in batches.

4. Return the onions and garlic to the pan, stirring continuously. Add the paprika, cumin, cloves, bay leaf and tomato purée. Cook for 2 minutes, then add the beef stock, stir well and bring to the boil.

5. Add the chickpeas and tinned tomatoes, and bring back to the boil. Reduce the heat to a simmer, cover with a lid and cook gently for 2 hours, stirring occasionally.

6. Put the peppers in a bowl, and add the remaining 2 tablespoons of olive oil, making sure the peppers are coated. Place on a roasting tray, skin side up, and cook in the oven for 15-20 minutes until the skins are blistered and lightly coloured. Put them back in the bowl and cover with cling film. Leave for 10-15 minutes, until they are cool enough to handle, then carefully peel away the skins and discard. Chop the peppers into small chunks and add to the soup.

7. Just before serving, check the meat is tender and adjust the seasoning if necessary. Stir in the chopped coriander, then serve in deep-sided bowls, garnishing with black olives and coriander leaves.

Fish Soup with Gruyère, Croutons and Rouille

Fish Soup with Gruyère, Croutons and Rouille

This recipe uses fish you may not have cooked before – gurnard, grey and red mullet – but they're easy to deal with as long as you ask your fishmonger to scale and fillet them, and to chop the bones into small pieces. Rouille is a rich garlic sauce – perfect for stirring into the soup.

Serves 6 45 mins preparation, 1 hour cooking

Ingredients

100ml olive oil
1 large onion, peeled and diced
1 bulb fennel, diced
4 cloves garlic, thinly sliced
2 sticks celery, diced
Zest of ½ orange
1 small bunch parsley stalks
2 bay leaves
1 pinch saffron filaments
½ red chilli, roughly chopped
100ml white wine
400g tinned chopped tomatoes
2 red peppers, deseeded and cut into quarters
Sea salt and milled black pepper
12 thin slices French bread
2 gurnard fillets
1 grey mullet fillet

1 red mullet fillet
400g cod fillet
100g Gruyère cheese, grated

For the rouille

2 slices white bread, soaked in cold water for 10 minutes
1 pinch saffron filaments, soaked in a tablespoon of warm water
2 cloves garlic, peeled and crushed
2 medium egg yolks
125ml olive oil
125ml vegetable oil
2 teaspoons lemon juice
1 teaspoon paprika

Baking tray
Food processor

1. Pre-heat the oven to 200°C/gas mark 6.

2. In a large saucepan over a medium heat, warm 50ml of the olive oil. Add the onion, fennel and garlic, and cook for 5-7 minutes without browning them. Stir in the celery, orange zest, parsley stalks, bay leaves, chilli, saffron and washed fish bones.

3. Sweat for 5 minutes, then add the white wine and bring to the boil. Cook for a further 2 minutes.

4. Add the tomatoes and enough water to cover. Bring to the boil and simmer for 30 minutes.

5. While the soup is cooking, rub the red peppers in a little olive oil, place on a baking sheet and roast in the oven for 20 minutes. Add them to the soup.

6. Allow the soup to cool slightly, then blitz in a food processor in small batches and force through a fine sieve into a clean pan. Check the seasoning, adding salt and pepper if necessary.

To make the rouille

1. Using your hands, squeeze the water from the soaked bread and place in a food processor, along with the saffron (including the water), garlic and egg yolks.

2. Blitz until smooth, and then slowly pour in both oils.

3. Finally add the lemon juice and paprika, and blend until all ingredients are fully combined.

To make the croutons

1. Heat the remaining olive oil in a large frying pan. Fry the French bread slices until crisp and golden on each side.

2. Drain on kitchen paper.

To serve

1. Bring the soup back to the boil and skim any oils from the surface.

2. Cut the fillets of fish into equally sized pieces and add to the soup. Simmer gently for 10 minutes, pour into soup bowls and serve with the French bread, grated Gruyère and rouille.

Celeriac and Smoked Bacon Soup

Celeriac and Smoked Bacon Soup

Celeriac is a wonderful winter vegetable, and works perfectly here with fennel, celery and thyme in a rich, creamy soup – all topped off with crispy smoked bacon.

Serves 6 15 mins preparation, 50 mins cooking

Ingredients
150g smoked bacon, diced
30g unsalted butter
2 onions, peeled and diced
1 teaspoon fennel seeds
1 small bulb fennel, peeled and diced
1 stick celery, peeled and diced
1 celeriac, peeled and diced
1 litre vegetable stock
2 sprigs fresh thyme
30ml double cream
Sea salt and milled black pepper

Food processor

1. Heat a large, heavy-bottomed pan, then add the smoked bacon and cook until crispy. Drain on kitchen roll and keep in a warm place.

2. Add the butter to the smoked bacon juices left in the pan. Heat until it's foaming, then add the onion and cook for 5 minutes, stirring until soft but not turning brown.

3. Add the fennel seeds, fennel, celery and celeriac and cook for 5 minutes.

4. Add the vegetable stock and thyme, and bring to the boil. Reduce the heat to a simmer and cook for 40 minutes.

5. Remove the soup from the heat, and blend in a food processor or liquidiser until smooth.

6. Pour into a clean pan, bring it back to the boil, and then reduce to a simmer. Stir in the cream and check the seasoning, adding salt and pepper if necessary. Pour the soup into bowls and sprinkle with the crispy smoked bacon.

Slow Cooked Recipes

Autumn and winter are all about stews and casseroles taking their time to simmer to perfection. I've included some British classics here, plus a few favourites from abroad – as well as a couple of puds that always benefit from the slow-cooking treatment.

Slow Cooking

Stews, hotpots, tagines, casseroles and traditional puddings. In recent years, slow cooking has become increasingly popular, for home cooks and restaurant chefs. With long hours of braising to develop deep, intense flavours, these dishes bring a feeling of homeliness to the kitchen. Warming and comforting, they are the perfect antidote to the chilly days and dark evenings of autumn and winter.

Slow cooking is also generally quite easy. Once you've done your preparation, and the pot's in the oven, you have plenty of time to get on with other parts of the meal. It's much more relaxing than having to stand over sizzling grills and bubbling pans, all demanding last-minute attention. In a way, these dishes look after themselves.

Another advantage of most slow-cooked recipes is they use cheaper cuts of meat. Lamb shanks or neck, pork shoulder and braising or stewing steak all transform from tough to tender with long, gentle cooking. Chicken and turkey work well too, especially on the bone. As long as you immerse them in enough liquid (usually stock or water), any of these budget-friendly meats will simmer away happily.

Try the slow-cooked recipes in this book, and you'll see how this simple method achieves wonderful results. But make sure your casserole dish has a well-fitting lid – to lock in all those mellow, reassuring flavours.

Steak and Ale Pudding

Serves 4 40 mins preparation, 3 hours 30 mins cooking

Ingredients

75g unsalted butter, plus extra for greasing
1 large onion, peeled and finely chopped
1kg stewing steak, diced
2 tablespoons plain flour
250g ox kidney, diced
250ml real ale
1 tablespoon tomato purée
350ml beef stock
1 teaspoon Worcestershire sauce

For the suet pastry

300g self-raising flour
150g suet
Sea salt and milled black pepper

Casserole dish
2 litre pudding basin
Steamer or large saucepan

To make the filling

1. Pre-heat the oven to 150°C/gas mark 2.

2. Melt the butter in a large casserole dish, add the onion and stir until lightly browned. Remove from the dish and keep to one side.

3. In a large bowl, mix the stewing steak with the plain flour to coat it thoroughly. Then brown the meat in batches, and let it rest with the onions. Flour, brown and rest the kidneys in the same way.

4. Add the ale to the casserole dish. Bring to a simmer, scraping any bits from the bottom. Add the tomato purée, stock and Worcestershire sauce, and then put the onions, steak and kidney back into the dish. Cover with a lid, and cook in the oven for 2 hours. Take the casserole out of the oven and let it cool completely.

To make the pastry

1. Mix the self-raising flour and suet in a large bowl, and season with salt and pepper. Using a fork, stir in enough water to make a soft dough. Flour a work surface, and divide the dough into a third and two thirds. Roll out the larger piece into a large circle.

2. Butter the pudding basin and line it with the pastry. Fill it with the cold, cooked meat mixture to within 2cm of the top.

3. Roll out the remaining pastry into a circle large enough to cover the top of the basin. Dampen the edges with a little water and place it over the pudding, as a lid. Gently press the pastry sides and lid together, then tie a pleated piece of greaseproof paper over the top of the basin. Then do the same with a sheet of tin foil.

To cook and serve

1. Use a steamer or a saucer placed upside down in the base of a large pan. Put the pudding basin inside and pour boiling water into the pan, halfway up the outside of the basin. Put the lid on, bring the water to the boil, and simmer gently for 1½ hours. Top up with boiling water when necessary.

2. Remove the basin from the water, and leave the pudding to rest for 10 minutes before turning it out onto a serving dish.

Steak and Ale Pudding

Hungarian Goulash

The key ingredient here is the paprika, which gives the goulash its distinctive flavour. For the meat, I use veal rather than beef – but always English rose veal, which is raised to high welfare standards and endorsed by the RSPCA.

Serves 6 30 mins preparation, 2 hours 30 mins cooking

Ingredients
1.5kg English rose veal shoulder
30g unsalted butter
2 tablespoons vegetable oil
2 large onions, peeled and chopped
4 cloves garlic, crushed
1½ tablespoons sweet paprika
1 teaspoon caraway seeds
1 bay leaf
400g tinned chopped tomatoes
1 tablespoon tomato purée
300ml beef stock

250ml red wine
2 red peppers, deseeded and thinly sliced
1 tablespoon red wine vinegar
Sea salt and milled black pepper

To serve
Buttered noodles
200ml soured cream

Casserole dish

1. Pre-heat the oven to 150°C/gas mark 2.

2. Trim any excess fat and sinew from the veal shoulder, and cut into small cubes.

3. Melt half the butter with the vegetable oil in a large, oven-proof pan or casserole dish. Over a high heat, brown the veal in batches, then remove from the pan and keep to one side.

4. Add the remaining butter and the onions to the pan, and cook for 5 minutes, stirring regularly. Add the garlic, paprika, caraway seeds and bay leaf, and cook for 2 minutes.

5. Return the meat to the pan, then add the tomatoes, tomato purée, beef stock, wine, peppers and vinegar. Bring to the boil, skimming off any sediment that has risen to the surface. Cover with a tight-fitting lid and cook in the oven for 1 hour.

6. Remove the lid and continue cooking for 1½ hours, stirring occasionally. By this time, the meat should be very tender. Check the seasoning, adding salt and pepper if necessary, and serve with buttered noodles and soured cream.

Hungarian Goulash

Beef Stew and Dumplings

Beef Stew and Dumplings

Serves 4 30 mins preparation, 2 hours 30 mins cooking

Ingredients
2 tablespoons plain flour
Sea salt and milled black pepper
750g stewing steak, diced
3 tablespoons vegetable oil
2 onions, peeled and chopped
3 carrots, peeled and chopped
¼ swede, peeled and chopped
500ml beef stock
3 sprigs fresh thyme
1 bay leaf
2 dashes Worcestershire sauce

For the dumplings
110g self-raising flour (plus a little extra
to form the dumplings)
50g beef suet
3 sprigs fresh thyme leaves
Sea salt and milled black pepper

To serve
Silky mashed potatoes (see page 90 for
my recipe)

Casserole dish

To make the beef stew

1. Pre-heat the oven to 160°C/gas mark 3.

2. Put the plain flour in a large bowl, and season well with salt and pepper. Add the steak, and mix to coat with flour.

3. Heat a large casserole dish over a high heat, and add the vegetable oil. When it's smoking, fry the beef in batches to seal – it should be nicely browned on all sides. Remove from the dish and put to one side.

4. Add the onions to the casserole dish, and cook for 5 minutes until soft. Add the carrot, swede, and then the sealed beef. Cover the meat and vegetables with the beef stock, topping up with water if necessary. Add the thyme, bay leaf and Worcestershire sauce, and bring to the boil.

5. Place the lid on the casserole, transfer it to the oven and cook for 2 hours, until the beef is tender.

To make the dumplings

1. In a large bowl, mix the self-raising flour, suet and thyme leaves, and season with salt and pepper. Add a little cold water and use a fork to mix the ingredients, until you have a light dough. Dip your hands in some extra flour and form balls with the dough, slightly smaller than a golf ball.

2. Remove the casserole from the oven. Give it a good stir and place the dumplings on top of the stew. Replace the lid and return the casserole to the oven for another 30 minutes, until the dumplings are light and fluffy. Serve with silky mashed potatoes.

Honey Roast Ham Hocks and Baked Beans

Honey Roast Ham Hocks and Baked Beans

Rich, sticky and satisfying, this dish certainly repays the time it takes to cook. When it's ready to serve, the ham is melting, and the beans have absorbed a wonderful cocktail of intense flavours. Don't forget to soak the beans overnight prior to starting this recipe!

Serves 4 20 mins preparation, 4 hours 20 mins cooking

Ingredients

2 tablespoons vegetable oil
1 large onion, peeled and finely chopped
2 ham hocks
1 bay leaf
3 litres cold water
500g dried haricot beans, soaked in a large pan of water overnight
1 tablespoon black treacle
75g soft brown sugar
5 tablespoons tomato purée

2 tablespoons Worcestershire sauce
1 teaspoon English mustard powder
2 teaspoons smoked paprika
4 cloves garlic, finely chopped
Sea salt and milled black pepper

Casserole dish

1. In a large casserole dish, heat the vegetable oil, then add the onions and cook until soft and golden. Add the ham hocks, bay leaf and water. Drain the soaked haricot beans and add them too. Bring to the boil, then reduce the heat and simmer for 1 hour.

2. Pre-heat the oven to 150°C/gas mark 2.

3. Strain the contents from the casserole dish through a colander into a large bowl. Pour 750ml of the strained liquid back into the casserole dish, and stir in the rest of the ingredients.

4. Return the beans and ham hocks to the casserole, and add enough of the remaining cooking liquid to cover the beans. Put the lid on the casserole dish and cook in the oven for 3 hours.

5. Carefully remove the ham hocks from the dish. Pull the meat off the bone, into small pieces, then return to the casserole dish. Cook without the lid for 20 minutes, until the sauce is thick and syrupy. Check the seasoning, adding salt and pepper if necessary, and serve.

Braised Short Rib of Beef with a Red Wine Reduction

Braised Short Rib of Beef with a Red Wine Reduction

Short rib is a meaty cut with loads of flavour that gets more intense over time. For best results, cook this dish (up to the point where you chill it) the day before you plan to serve it.

Serves 6 40 mins preparation, 3 hours 40 mins cooking

Ingredients
2kg short rib of beef
Sea salt and milled black pepper
2 tablespoons plain flour
2 onions, peeled and roughly chopped
3 carrots, peeled and roughly chopped
3 sticks celery, roughly chopped
1 leek, roughly chopped
½ bulb garlic
3 sprigs fresh thyme
1 litre beef stock

For the red wine reduction
750ml red wine (preferably cabernet sauvignon)
1 onion, peeled and diced
2 carrots, peeled and diced
2 shallots, peeled and diced
1 leek, diced
100g button mushrooms, sliced
3 sprigs fresh thyme
2 bay leaves
3 cloves garlic

Casserole dish

To serve
Roast autumn roots, sage and maple glaze
(see page 88 for my recipe)

1. Combine all the red wine reduction ingredients in a casserole dish large enough to take the beef ribs later. Bring to the boil, then turn the heat down to a slow simmer and cook for 40 minutes, until the wine has reduced to a glaze.

2. Pre-heat the oven to 180°C/gas mark 4.

3. Season all sides of the meat with salt and pepper and dust with plain flour. Heat a large frying pan and sear the meat until golden brown on all sides.

4. Add the rest of the ingredients to the red wine reduction. Mix together, then carefully add the seared beef. It needs to be fully covered, so add water if required. Place a tight-fitting lid onto the dish, bring back to a simmer, and transfer to the oven. Cook for 2-2 ½ hours, until the beef is tender and falling apart.

5. Transfer the meat to a large bowl, and pass the stock twice through a fine sieve. Leave to settle, skimming any fat off the surface. Pour back over the beef and leave to cool, then chill it in the fridge until you need it (it can keep for up to 3 days).

6. To finish the dish, pre-heat the oven to 190°C/gas mark 5. Lift the beef out of the stock and cut it into serving sized portions. Remove any fat from the surface of the stock.

7. Place the stock in a casserole dish and bring to the boil. Reduce to a sticky consistency, then add the beef and bring back to a simmer.

8. Baste the juices over the beef, then transfer the uncovered casserole dish to the oven and cook for 20 minutes, basting from time to time.

9. Turn the meat over and return to the oven for 10 minutes. The meat should be hot, richly browned, with a sticky sauce. Serve with roast autumn roots, sage and maple glaze.

Coq au Vin

Serves 4 40 mins preparation, 1 hour 30 mins cooking, 12 hours marinating

Ingredients

3 tablespoons olive oil
2 small onions, peeled and diced
2 sticks celery, diced
2 carrots, peeled and diced
2 bay leaves
Small bunch fresh thyme
750ml red wine
1.5kg whole chicken, cut into eight pieces
200g pancetta, diced
25g unsalted butter
12 small shallots, peeled

150g button mushrooms
25g plain flour
500ml chicken stock

To serve

Silky mashed potatoes
(see page 90 for my recipe)

Casserole dish

1. Heat a large saucepan, and add 1 tablespoon of olive oil. Add the onions, celery, carrots, bay leaves and thyme, and cook for 5 minutes, stirring occasionally.

2. Add the red wine and bring to the boil. Remove from the heat and leave to cool.

3. When cool, add the chicken pieces and cover with cling film. Leave to marinate in the fridge for at least 12 hours.

4. Bring a pan of water to the boil, add the pancetta and simmer gently for 5 minutes. Drain, and dry on kitchen paper.

5. Heat a frying pan, add the pancetta and cook until crispy. Then remove from the pan and keep to one side.

6. Using the same pan, add half the butter and the shallots, and cook until browned on all sides. Remove them from the pan and keep to one side. Add the remaining butter and cook the mushrooms for 5 minutes. Remove and keep these to one side as well.

7. Drain the marinated chicken and vegetables into a colander, over a bowl to save the marinade. Take out the chicken, pat dry on kitchen paper and coat in flour.

8. Heat a large casserole dish and pour in the remaining olive oil. Add the chicken and cook until golden on all sides, then add the marinade and chicken stock and bring to the boil. Reduce the heat to a simmer, put the lid on the casserole, and cook for 45 minutes.

9. If the sauce is a little thin, remove the chicken and keep in a warm place, then increase the heat and reduce the sauce to the consistency you prefer.

10. Return the chicken pieces to the casserole, then add the cooked pancetta, shallots and mushrooms. Bring it all back to the boil, and simmer gently for 10 minutes. Serve with silky mashed potatoes.

Coq au Vin

Lancashire Hotpot

Lancashire Hotpot

A hearty, slow-cooked classic, this is a meal in itself, as all the potatoes and veg are included. It's such a great dish, we even eat it in Yorkshire!

Serves 4 30 mins preparation, 1 hour 30 mins cooking

Ingredients

2 tablespoons olive oil
1kg neck fillet of lamb, trimmed and diced
1 tablespoon plain flour
1 litre beef stock
3 large onions, peeled and thinly sliced
4 carrots, peeled and sliced
2 cloves garlic, peeled and finely chopped
2 sticks celery, diced

4 sprigs fresh thyme leaves
Sea salt and milled black pepper
4 medium Maris Piper potatoes, peeled and thinly sliced
25g unsalted butter, diced

Casserole dish

1. Heat a large casserole dish over a high heat. When it's smoking, add a tablespoon of olive oil and brown the lamb in batches, removing each batch from the pan and keeping to one side.

2. When you've sealed all the meat, return it to the casserole dish. Add the flour and stir for a few minutes. Slowly add the stock, bring to the boil and simmer gently for 30 minutes.

3. Meanwhile, pour the remaining olive oil into a heavy-bottomed pan over a high heat. When it's smoking, add the onions, then stir and cook for 5 minutes. Reduce the heat, cover with a lid and cook gently for another 15-20 minutes until the onions are lightly coloured and slightly sticky.

4. Pre-heat the oven to 180°C/gas mark 4.

5. Add the carrots, garlic and celery to the lamb, and cook for a further 10 minutes. Take it off the heat, then stir in the onions and thyme. Check the seasoning, adding salt and pepper if necessary.

6. Arrange the potatoes over the top, pressing each layer lightly to submerge them in the pan juices. Scatter the butter over the top, cover with the casserole lid and bake in the oven for 40 minutes. Serve the hotpot simply by itself.

Butternut Squash Filled with Roast Roots, Plum Purée and Celeriac Cream

Ripe butternut squash has a lovely sweetness, and the maple-roasted roots and plum purée bring this out beautifully.

Serves 4 40 mins preparation, 1 hour 20 mins cooking

Ingredients
4 butternut squash (as large and round as possible)
Sea salt and milled black pepper
40g unsalted butter
1 celeriac, peeled and halved
50ml double cream
2 parsnips, peeled and cut into small, equally sized wedges
4 carrots, peeled and cut into small, equally sized wedges
½ swede, peeled and cut into small, equally sized wedges
100ml rapeseed oil
1 tablespoon maple syrup
20 fresh sage leaves

For the plum purée
200g Victoria plums
2 tablespoons demerara sugar
2 star anise
½ cinnamon stick

Ovenproof dish
Food processor
Roasting tray

To make the plum purée

1. Pre-heat the oven to 160°C/gas mark 3.

2. Halve the plums and remove the stones. Place them in a small ovenproof dish, sprinkle with demerara sugar, then add the star anise and cinnamon. Cover the dish with tin foil and roast for 20 minutes, until the plums are soft.

3. Discard the star anise and cinnamon, and blitz the plums in a food processor until smooth. Pour the purée into a small pan and keep in a warm place.

Butternut Squash Filled with Roast Roots, Plum Purée and Celeriac Cream

To make the filled squash

1. Pre-heat the oven to 200°C/gas mark 6.

2. Peel the butternut squash. Cut the top halves off, saving them for later, and scoop out and discard the seeds.

3. Stand the squash bases on a roasting tray, season them with salt and pepper, and put 10g of butter in each hollow. Cover with tin foil and roast for 30 minutes.

4. Using a pointed knife, check the squash are tender, then remove from the oven and keep in a warm place.

5. Take one celeriac half and chop into small pieces. Place in a pan with water and season with a little salt. Bring to the boil, then reduce the heat to a simmer and cook for 15 to 20 minutes, until tender. Strain through a colander.

6. In a small pan, bring the double cream to the boil. Then reduce the heat and simmer gently for 2 minutes to reduce it slightly.

7. Place the cooked celeriac in a food processor, add the cream and blend until smooth. Keep in a warm place.

8. Cut the remaining half of celeriac and tops of the butternut squash into similar sized wedges as before. Place these on a roasting tray with the parsnips, carrots and swede, and drizzle with rapeseed oil. Season lightly with salt and pepper, and roast for 25 minutes until tender.

9. Add the maple syrup and sage leaves, then cook to caramelise for a further 10 minutes. At the same time, return the butternut bases to the oven and carefully reheat the celeriac cream.

10. To serve, fill the 4 butternut bases with the roast roots. Place each one on a plate, drizzle with the plum purée, and serve the celeriac cream on the side.

Lamb and Apricot Tagine

Lamb and Apricot Tagine

This Moroccan dish is a brilliant example of how slow cooking lets flavours combine and develop. All the spices, fruit and ginger penetrate deep into the meat, and create a rich, vibrant sauce.

Serves 6 40 mins preparation, 2 hours 30 mins cooking

Ingredients

3 tablespoons olive oil
1.5kg neck of lamb, trimmed and cut into large pieces
2 medium onions, peeled and chopped
4 cloves garlic, peeled and finely chopped
2 teaspoons ground coriander
2 teaspoons ground cumin
1 teaspoon ground cinnamon
1 teaspoon ground turmeric
1 teaspoon paprika
½ teaspoon cayenne pepper
1 tablespoon tomato purée
2 tablespoons ground almonds
Zest of ½ orange

20g fresh ginger, grated
400ml chicken stock
150g semi-dried apricots, halved
3 tablespoons fresh coriander, chopped, plus a few extra leaves for garnish
Sea salt and milled black pepper
2 tablespoons toasted flaked almonds

To serve

Couscous

Casserole dish

1. Pre-heat the oven to 170°C/gas mark 3.

2. Heat a large casserole dish, add 2 tablespoons of olive oil and brown the lamb in batches. Remove from the pan and keep to one side.

3. Heat the remaining oil, add the onions and garlic, and cook for 4-5 minutes. Stir in all the spices, and cook for a further 5 minutes.

4. Add the tomato purée, ground almonds, orange zest and ginger. Return the lamb to the casserole dish, cover with chicken stock, and bring to the boil. Cover with a tight-fitting lid and cook in the oven for 2 hours.

5. Remove from the oven, and give it a good stir. Add the apricots and chopped coriander.

6. Remove the lid and place the casserole dish on the hob. Bring to the boil and simmer gently to reduce the sauce, stirring occasionally. Be very careful not to burn the base of the casserole dish. Check the seasoning, adding salt and pepper if necessary, then garnish with a scatter of toasted almonds and coriander leaves. Serve with couscous.

Creamed Rice Pudding and Autumn Fruits

Creamed Rice Pudding and Autumn Fruits

Homemade rice pudding is well worth taking the extra time for – and the preparation is very easy. You can serve it with stewed fruit as I suggest here – or simply dig in with a large spoon!

Serves 4   10 mins preparation, 1 hour 10 mins cooking

Ingredients
750ml full fat milk
300ml double cream
100g caster sugar
100g short grain or pudding rice
1 teaspoon vanilla extract
⅓ of a whole nutmeg, grated

Baking dish

For the autumn fruits
12 Victoria Plums, halved and stone removed
3 tablespoons soft brown sugar
30g unsalted butter, diced
2 star anise
½ cinnamon stick
3 tablespoons dark rum

To make the rice pudding

1. Pre-heat the oven to 150°C/gas mark 2.

2. Place the milk, cream, sugar, rice and vanilla into a large, heavy-bottomed saucepan. Over a medium heat, bring the pan to the boil, then turn down the heat and simmer gently for 30 minutes, stirring from time to time.

3. For the last 5 minutes of this stage, stir continuously to prevent the rice from sticking to the pan.

To make the autumn fruits

1. Pre-heat the oven to 180°C/gas mark 4.

2. Spread a large sheet of tin foil on a work surface, and lay a square of baking parchment on top. Place the plums on the parchment, cut side up, and sprinkle with the brown sugar and butter. Add the star anise and cinnamon, and sprinkle with the rum.

3. Gather the sides of the tin foil and scrunch together into a sealed parcel. Place this onto a baking tray and bake for 20 minutes, then set aside to cool.

To serve

1. Pour the pudding into a baking dish and grate the nutmeg over the top. Bake for 40 minutes, then leave it to stand in a warm place for 1 hour. Serve slightly warm with stewed autumn fruits.

Bread and Butter Pudding

Bread and Butter Pudding

I think this will always be a family favourite – and rightly so. Breaking through the crispy caramelised top into the soft, creamy centre is a pleasure that brings back the best childhood memories.

Serves 6 15 mins preparation, 50 mins cooking

Ingredients
8 slices slightly stale white bread
75g unsalted butter
100g sultanas
220ml full fat milk
220ml double cream
50g caster sugar
1 vanilla pod
4 medium egg yolks
50g apricot jam
25g icing sugar

To serve
Clotted cream

Baking dish which fits into a deep sided tin

1. Pre-heat the oven to 150°C/gas mark 2.

2. Remove the crusts from the bread, butter each slice and cut into 4 triangles. Place a layer of bread in the bottom of your baking dish and sprinkle with a layer of sultanas. Repeat this with the remaining bread and sultanas.

3. In a large, heavy saucepan, mix the milk, cream and sugar. Split the vanilla pod in half lengthways, scrape the seeds into the mixture and bring to the boil.

4. In a large bowl, whisk the egg yolks. Then, a little at a time, pour the cream mixture over, whisking continuously.

5. Pour the mixture over the bread and place the dish in a large, deep-sided tin. Pour boiling water into the tin around the pudding, until it's three quarters full. Bake in the oven for 40 minutes, then let it rest in a warm place.

6. In a small saucepan, gently warm the apricot jam. Dust the pudding with icing sugar and caramelise under a hot grill or using a blowtorch. Brush the top of the pudding with the apricot jam, and serve with clotted cream.

Autumn classics

So many fantastic ingredients are at their best in the autumn –
especially game and our local varieties of fruit and vegetables.
I've made the most of them with these classic recipes, all
designed for informal entertaining.

Smoked Haddock and Welsh Rarebit

The distinctive flavour of smoked haddock stands up well to the richness and bite of this rarebit topping – and the tomatoes bring a fresh lightness.

Serves 4 15 mins preparation, 30 mins cooking

Ingredients

500ml milk
50g unsalted butter
50g plain flour
70ml beer (dark ale is ideal)
20g English mustard
1 teaspoon Worcestershire sauce
350g mature Cheddar, grated

2 large fillets of natural (undyed) smoked haddock, halved
4 ripe tomatoes, thinly sliced

To serve
Green salad

1. In a small saucepan, bring 200ml of milk to the boil.

2. In a second pan, melt the butter, stir in the flour and mix into a roux. Cook gently for a few minutes, then add the hot milk, a little at a time, stirring until smooth between each addition.

3. Add the beer, mustard and Worcestershire sauce. Remove the pan from the heat, then stir in the cheese until it's melted and smooth. This is your rarebit – set aside in a warm place until you need it.

4. Place the haddock fillets in a large pan and cover with the remaining milk. If the fillets are not covered, top up with cold water. Over a medium heat, bring to the boil and simmer for 2-3 minutes, then remove the pan from the heat and let it rest for 5 minutes.

5. Pre-heat the grill to the highest setting.

6. Arrange a fan of tomatoes for each haddock on a serving plate. Carefully lift the haddock fillets out of the pan, letting any excess liquid escape, and place on top of the tomatoes.

7. Divide the rarebit mixture into four and spread over the top of each piece of haddock. Place under the grill until golden brown, and serve with a green salad.

Smoked Haddock and Welsh Rarebit

Roast Loin of Pork with Cinnamon and Apple

If you like roast pork with apple, try this version. The cinnamon really lifts the flavours of the meat, blending perfectly with the buttery apple rings.

Serves 8 20 mins preparation, 1 hour 30 mins cooking

Ingredients

1.5kg traditionally bred pork loin (ask your butcher to score the rind)
1½ cinnamon sticks
1 tablespoon sea salt
3 Granny Smith apples
25g unsalted butter
1 tablespoon sugar
Juice of ½ lemon

12 sage leaves
2 tablespoons plain flour
500ml boiling water

To serve
Seasonal vegetables

Roasting tin

1. Remove the pork loin from the fridge and leave at room temperature for 1 hour before cooking.

2. Pre-heat the oven to 220°C/gas mark 7.

3. Place the pork, rind side up in a colander, hold over the sink and pour boiling water over the rind.

4. Pat the pork dry with kitchen paper, then place in a roasting tin.

5. Roast the pork for 20 minutes, then reduce the temperature to 180°C/gas mark 4.

6. Break the cinnamon sticks into fragments, mix with the sea salt and sprinkle this over the pork. Continue cooking for 1 hour.

7. While the pork is roasting, core the apples, remove the top and bottom, and cut each one into 4 equal rings. Heat a large frying pan and add the butter. When it starts to foam, add the apple rings, sprinkle with the sugar and cook until golden on each side. Add the lemon juice, sprinkle with sage leaves and keep warm until required.

8. When the pork has finished cooking, take it out of the roasting tin and rest in a warm place.

9. To make a gravy, pour the excess fat from the roasting tin into a small bowl, then mix with the plain flour until it forms a smooth roux. Add 500ml boiling water to the roasting tin, then bring to the boil on the hob and use a spoon to loosen any sediment from the bottom of the tin. Whisk in the flour roux, a little at a time, until you have the right thickness. Strain the gravy and put to one side.

10. To serve, carve the pork into thick slices, and serve with the apple rings, gravy and seasonal vegetables.

Roast Loin of Pork with Cinnamon and Apple

Pan Roast Rack of Venison with Chocolate Sauce

Pan Roast Rack of Venison with Chocolate Sauce

One of the great joys of autumn is all the wonderful game that's in season. Venison is a favourite because it's so lean – and with this sticky, satisfying red wine and chocolate sauce, it makes a really warming supper dish.

Serves 4 30 mins preparation, 3 hours cooking

Ingredients

500g venison bones
4 tablespoons olive oil
1 carrot, peeled and diced
1 onion, peeled and diced
1 clove garlic, roughly chopped
1 stick celery, roughly chopped
500ml beef stock
6 juniper berries, crushed
1 bay leaf
1 sprig thyme
100ml port
250ml red wine
8 bone rack of venison

Sea salt and milled black pepper
30g chocolate (70% cocoa solids), chopped into small pieces
1 teaspoon raspberry vinegar

To serve

Seasonal vegetables

Roasting tin

1. Pre-heat the oven to 200°C/gas mark 6.

2. Place the venison bones in a large roasting tin, and roast for 30 minutes.

3. Heat a large, heavy pan. Add 2 tablespoons of olive oil, then the carrot, onion, garlic and celery, and fry very gently for 3-4 minutes.

4. Add the roast venison bones, and cook for a further 5 minutes.

5. Add the beef stock, juniper berries, bay leaf and thyme. The bones should be covered – if not, add some water.

6. Bring to the boil, then simmer gently for 2 hours, skimming any fats from the top of the stock.

7. Pass the stock through a fine sieve into a clean pan. Bring it back to the boil and keep cooking until you've reduced the volume by half.

8. Heat a second heavy pan. When it starts to smoke, add the port and reduce it by half, then add the red wine and keep reducing until you have the consistency of a syrup. Finally add the venison stock and reduce by half until you have a nice, concentrated sauce. Keep this until you need it. You can make the sauce a day in advance and keep it in the fridge.

9. Heat a large frying pan over a high heat. Rub the rack of venison with the remaining olive oil, and season with salt and pepper. Once the pan is hot and starting to smoke, fry the venison for 1-2 minutes on each side, until completely sealed.

10. Transfer the venison to a roasting tray, and roast it in the oven – for 20 minutes if you like it pink, or for 25-30 minutes for medium. Remove it from the oven, cover with tin foil, and let it rest in a warm place for 15-20 minutes.

11. Reheat your sauce until it's boiling, then let it simmer gently while you carve the venison.

12. At the last minute, remove the sauce from the heat and use a whisk to melt in the chopped chocolate and raspberry vinegar. Do this very quickly, and don't put the sauce back on the heat. You should now have a very smooth, silky, rich sauce. Pour it around the venison, and serve with seasonal vegetables.

Roast Partridge with Pancetta and Braised Cabbage

Partridge makes a tasty change from chicken – and as each person gets a whole bird, this is a great dinner party dish.

Serves 4 30 mins preparation, 35 mins cooking

Ingredients

30g unsalted butter
4 oven-ready partridge
4 sprigs fresh thyme
8 thin slices streaky bacon
2 tablespoons vegetable oil
200g pancetta, diced
1 onion, peeled and finely chopped
2 sticks celery, finely chopped
1 large carrot, peeled and finely chopped

1 teaspoon fresh thyme leaves
1 small Savoy cabbage (outer leaves removed), quartered, cored and finely shredded
100ml double cream

Roasting tray
Casserole dish

1. Pre-heat the oven to 220°C/gas mark 7.

2. Smear butter over each partridge, place a sprig of thyme over the breast and wrap two slices of streaky bacon over the top of each bird.

3. Place all four in a large roasting tray and roast for 10 minutes.

4. Reduce the heat to 180°C/gas mark 4 and cook for a further 20 minutes.

5. While the partridge are roasting, heat a large casserole dish over a high heat, then add the vegetable oil and pancetta, stirring until it's coloured and lightly crisp. Transfer it from the pan to a warm dish, using a slotted spoon, and keep it in a warm place.

6. Add the chopped onion to the casserole dish, and cook for 2-3 minutes before adding the celery, carrot and thyme leaves. Cook for a further 2 minutes before adding the shredded cabbage. Stir for 4-5 minutes, reduce the heat, then place a lid over the casserole. Cook for 20 minutes, stirring occasionally.

7. When the partridge have finished roasting, remove the tray from the oven. Cover with tin foil and rest in a warm place for 10 minutes.

8. Add the pancetta and cream to the braised cabbage and season with salt and pepper.

9. To serve, place a mound of cabbage in the centre of a warmed plate, sit the rested partridge on top and pour the pan roasting juices over each one.

Roast Partridge with Pancetta and Braised Cabbage

Warm Roast Pigeon with Beetroot Salad

Warm Roast Pigeon with Beetroot Salad

It's the roast pigeon that makes this salad warm – and the rich, gamey meat goes beautifully with the beetroot, feta and hazelnuts.

Serves 4 20 mins preparation, 10 mins cooking

Ingredients
30g Dijon mustard
50ml white wine vinegar
Sea salt and milled black pepper
200ml sunflower oil
50g rocket leaves
1 bunch watercress
4 breasts wood pigeon
1 tablespoon olive oil
20g unsalted butter
2 medium-sized cooked beetroot, peeled and diced
100g barrel-aged Greek feta cheese (normal feta can be used as an alternative)
2 tablespoons crushed, roasted hazelnuts

1. In a bowl, whisk the mustard and vinegar with a pinch of salt and pepper. Slowly pour in the sunflower oil, whisking until it makes a smooth dressing. Put it to one side – you won't need all of it for this recipe, so keep the rest in a sealed container for another time.

2. Wash the rocket and watercress leaves, drain in a colander and put to one side.

3. Season the pigeon breasts on both sides. Heat a large, heavy-bottomed frying pan, and when it's smoking, add the olive oil and butter, followed by the pigeon breasts. Cook for 3-4 minutes on each side. Remove from the pan and let them rest for 10 minutes in a warm place.

4. Divide the rocket and watercress between 4 plates, then scatter the beetroot on top. Carve the pigeon breast into thin slices and arrange it on each salad. Crumble the feta cheese over, sprinkle with hazelnuts, then drizzle with the dressing and serve.

Coquilles St Jacques

Serves 4 1 hour preparation, 15-20 mins cooking

Ingredients

250ml milk
½ small onion, peeled and chopped
4 black peppercorns
4 cloves
1 bay leaf
25g unsalted butter
25g plain flour
50ml white wine
2 shallots, finely chopped
100g button mushrooms, thinly sliced
100ml double cream

Sea salt and milled black pepper
4 medium Maris Piper potatoes, peeled and diced
1 egg yolk
6 fresh large king scallops
125g Cheddar cheese, grated
2 tablespoons breadcrumbs

Piping bag
4 king scallop shells (or ovenproof serving bowls)

1. Place the milk, onion, peppercorns, cloves and bay leaf in a saucepan. Bring to the boil, then remove from the heat and keep to one side.

2. In a second saucepan, melt the butter, add the plain flour and mix into a roux. Cook this gently for 2-3 minutes.

3. Strain the milk mixture through a sieve and pour a little at a time into the roux, mixing thoroughly after each addition. Continue until you have a smooth béchamel sauce. Reduce the heat to low, and cook the sauce gently for 20 minutes, stirring occasionally.

4. In another saucepan, heat the white wine, shallots and mushrooms. Bring to the boil and keep cooking until you've reduced the volume by half. Add 50ml of the double cream, and reduce further to a thick sauce.

5. Remove this sauce from the heat and add to the béchamel sauce. Check the seasoning, adding salt and pepper if necessary, then cover with a sheet of cling film to prevent a skin forming.

6. Pre-heat the oven to 200°C/gas mark 6.

7. Place the potatoes in a pan, cover with water, bring to the boil and cook until tender. Strain and mash until smooth.

8. Allow the potatoes to cool slightly before mixing in the egg yolk and remaining double cream. Season with salt and pepper, place into a piping bag with a star nozzle, and pipe the mash around the inside edges of each scallop shell.

9. Cut each scallop into four even slices.

10. Place a good spoonful of sauce in the base of each shell then fan six slices of scallop on top. Cover completely with more sauce, and sprinkle the grated Cheddar over each shell, followed by the breadcrumbs.

11. Place the shells on a baking tray and cook on the top shelf of the oven for 15-20 minutes, until golden brown. If they do not colour, finish them under a hot grill before serving.

Coquilles St Jacques

Pumpkin Risotto

Serves 4-6 30 mins preparation, 50 mins cooking

Ingredients

1kg pumpkin, peeled, deseeded and diced
50g unsalted butter, diced
2 bunches fresh sage
Sea salt and milled black pepper
1.2 litres vegetable stock
2 tablespoons olive oil

2 shallots, finely chopped
1 small clove garlic, peeled and finely chopped
500g Arborio rice
150ml white wine
75g Parmesan cheese, grated

1. Pre-heat the oven to 180°C/gas mark 4.

2. Spread a large sheet of tin foil on a work surface, and lay a smaller piece of baking parchment on top. Put the diced pumpkin on the parchment, and sprinkle with the butter, along with half the sage leaves. Season with a little salt and pepper.

3. Pull up the sides of the tin foil and scrunch together into a parcel. Place this on a baking sheet and bake in the oven for 20-25 minutes.

4. Meanwhile, heat the vegetable stock and bring to a simmer.

5. In a large, heavy-bottomed pan, heat the olive oil. When it's hot, add the remaining sage leaves and cook for about 1 minute, until lightly crisp. Carefully place them on some kitchen paper, sprinkle with a little salt and set aside.

6. Using the same pan with the remaining olive oil, add the shallots and garlic, and cook for a few minutes, stirring constantly until soft.

7. Add the rice and cook for 2 more minutes, stirring until it becomes shiny and translucent.

8. Add the white wine, then increase the heat and let the liquid reduce to nothing.

9. Add a ladle full of hot stock, stirring until the rice has absorbed it. Repeat this with the remaining stock, adding a little at a time; this will take 15-20 minutes.

10. Check the rice is cooked by tasting a few grains. If it's crunchy on the outside, cook it for a few more minutes. Remove it from the heat.

11. Take the pumpkin parcel out of the oven. Check it's cooked, then discard the sage leaves and pour the pumpkin and juices into the rice. Stir well, and add the Parmesan.

12. Adjust the seasoning if necessary, and serve the risotto in warm, shallow bowls with the crisp sage leaves sprinkled on top.

Pumpkin Risotto

Seafood Thermidor

Seafood Thermidor

Serves 4 1 hour 15 mins preparation, 30 mins cooking

Ingredients

400ml milk
400ml fish stock
75g unsalted butter
75g plain flour
100ml double cream
3 shallots, finely diced
150g button mushrooms, thinly sliced
175ml white wine
1 tablespoon English mustard
150g Cheddar cheese, grated
400g salmon fillet
300g cod or haddock fillet

250g monkfish fillet
250g halibut fillet
12 shelled tiger prawn tails
Sea salt and milled black pepper
4 tablespoons brandy
30g breadcrumbs

To serve
Crusty bread

4 Ovenproof dishes

1. In a small saucepan, bring the milk and fish stock to a simmer, then remove from the heat and keep warm.

2. In a second, heavy-bottomed pan, melt the butter. When it's foaming, stir in the flour for 3-4 minutes to make a roux.

3. Slowly add the milk stock to the roux, a ladle at a time, stirring after each addition until you have a smooth sauce. Stir in the cream, reduce the heat and cook gently for 20 minutes to make a white sauce.

4. In a small pan, add the shallots, mushrooms and white wine. Bring to the boil and cook until the wine has reduced by half. Strain it through a sieve, keeping the shallots and mushrooms to one side and adding the remaining wine liquor to the white sauce.

5. Bring the sauce back to the boil, then remove from the heat. Add the mustard and half of the grated cheese, stirring until the sauce is smooth.

6. Pre-heat the oven to 180°C/gas mark 4.

7. Cut the fillets of fish into thin, equally sized strips, around 1cm thick. Divide these between 4 ovenproof dishes, then split the tiger prawns in half and add to the fish.

8. Lightly season the seafood with salt and pepper, then scatter the mushrooms and shallots over the top. Sprinkle with brandy and pour the sauce over each dish to cover the fish. Sprinkle with the remaining grated cheese and breadcrumbs.

9. Bake in the oven for 30 minutes until bubbling and golden brown. Serve simply with crusty bread.

Roast Butternut Wedges with Hazelnuts, Goats' Cheese and Pesto

Roast Butternut Wedges with Hazelnuts, Goats' Cheese and Pesto

Serves 4 20 mins preparation, 20 mins cooking

Ingredients
1 butternut squash, peeled, deseeded and cut into 6 wedges
4 tablespoons olive oil
½ teaspoon ground cumin
½ teaspoon dried chilli flakes
½ teaspoon sea salt
Milled black pepper
1 large bunch fresh rocket
120g soft goats' cheese
2 tablespoons roasted hazelnuts, lightly crushed

For the pesto
2 large bunches basil leaves
50g toasted pine nuts
70g Parmesan cheese, grated
100ml olive oil
Pinch sea salt
Milled black pepper

Food processor
Roasting tray

To make the pesto

1. Place the basil leaves, pine nuts and Parmesan into a food processor, and pulse.

2. Slowly add the olive oil until it forms a paste. Season with salt and pepper, and keep in a sealed jar in the fridge until you need it.

To make the wedges

1. Pre-heat the oven to 220°C/gas mark 7.

2. Place the butternut squash in a large bowl. Drizzle with 2 tablespoons of olive oil, then add the cumin, chilli flakes, salt and pepper. Mix well and tip onto a roasting tray, spreading it out in a single layer.

3. Roast the squash for 10 minutes until tender and lightly coloured on the edges.

To serve

1. Divide the squash between 4 plates.

2. Scatter the rocket leaves on top, then crumble the goats' cheese over and sprinkle on the hazelnuts.

3. Drizzle with the pesto and a little olive oil.

Melting Chocolate Fondant

Creating these moist dark chocolate puddings with a gooey melting centre is easier than it looks. Follow these quantities and timings, and you'll see impressive results.

Serves 6 20 mins preparation, 10 mins cooking, 1 hour 20 mins chilling

Ingredients
90g softened unsalted butter, plus a little extra for greasing the rings
90g dark chocolate (70% cocoa solids), finely chopped
2 medium eggs
2 medium egg yolks
120g caster sugar
45g plain flour, sieved

To serve
Vanilla ice cream

6 metal rings

1. Pre-heat the oven to 180°C/gas mark 4.

2. Butter the inside of the metal rings, and line each one with non-stick baking parchment to come just above the top. Stand them on a parchment-lined baking tray.

3. Melt the chocolate very gently in a bowl over a pan of hot water. Add the butter and stir until thoroughly mixed.

4. In a separate bowl, whisk the eggs, egg yolks and sugar until evenly combined. Mix in the melted chocolate, and gently fold in the flour. Chill in the fridge for 20 minutes.

5. Spoon the mixture into the parchment-lined rings, until they are about two thirds full. Chill them in the fridge for at least an hour (they will keep for up to 6 hours).

6. To bake the fondants, place the tray in the centre of the oven and cook for 10 minutes. Let them rest for 2 minutes before carefully lifting away the metal rings and parchment. Transfer them to small serving plates and serve with vanilla ice cream.

Melting Chocolate Fondant

Apple Pie

Apple Pie

I'm sure homemade apple pie must be high on most people's list of favourite comfort foods. Here we use a mix of cooking and eating apples, for extra texture and taste.

Serves 6-8 30 mins preparation, 1 hour cooking, 1 hour 30 mins chilling

Ingredients
For the pastry
230g plain flour
150g chilled unsalted butter, diced
Zest of 1 lemon
75g caster sugar
1 medium egg and 1 medium egg yolk,
beaten together

For the filling
25g unsalted butter
5 Bramley cooking apples, peeled, cored
and thinly sliced
150g caster sugar, plus extra for dusting
3 eating apples, peeled, cored and
thinly sliced
2 tablespoons milk

To serve
Double cream, vanilla ice cream or, if
you're in Yorkshire, Wensleydale cheese

20cm loose-bottomed flan tin, 5cm deep

To make the pastry

1. Place the flour and butter in a large bowl, and gently work them together until the mix resembles breadcrumbs.

2. Stir in the lemon zest and sugar, then slowly mix in the eggs to form a dough.

3. Shape the dough into a ball, wrap it in cling film and keep in the fridge for 1 hour

4. On a floured surface, roll out two thirds of the pastry until it's 5mm thick. Then use it to line the flan tin, very carefully, letting the pastry hang over the sides.

5. Put the tin on a baking tray and keep it in the fridge for another 30 minutes.

6. Place the remaining pastry between two floured sheets of baking parchment and roll this to form the pie lid. Put this in the fridge for 30 minutes too.

To make the filling

1. Melt the butter in a large, heavy pan over a medium heat. Add the cooking apples and sugar, then cover with a lid and cook gently for 10-15 minutes, stirring occasionally.

2. Mix the eating apples in with the cooked apples, then spread them onto a large tray to cool.

To assemble and bake the pie

1. Pre-heat the oven to 180°C/gas mark 4.

2. Remove the lined pastry tin from the fridge and fill it carefully with the apple mixture.

3. Brush the edges of the pastry with a little milk, and place the pastry lid on top. Press the lid gently around the edges to seal it, and trim off the excess pastry.

4. Cut two slits in the centre of the lid, brush it with the remaining milk and sprinkle with the extra caster sugar.

5. Bake the pie for 50-55 minutes until it's a nice, golden colour.

To serve

1. Let the pie rest for 15 minutes before removing it from the tin.

2. Serve with double cream or vanilla ice cream – or Wensleydale cheese (a Yorkshire classic).

Slow Roast Spiced Plums and Vanilla Panna Cotta

Slow Roast Spiced Plums and Vanilla Panna Cotta

Literally 'cooked cream', panna cotta is a classic Italian dessert that works best with fruits that balance its richness. So tangy plums are the perfect partner – especially when they're baked with cinnamon and rum.

Serves 6 20 mins preparation, 30 mins cooking, 3-4 hours chilling

Ingredients
For the panna cotta
330ml double cream
50ml full fat milk
50g caster sugar
1 vanilla pod
1½ leaves gelatine
1 teaspoon dark rum

6 ramekin dishes

For the spiced plums
12 Victoria plums, cut in half and stone removed
3 tablespoons soft brown sugar
30g unsalted butter, diced
2 star anise
½ cinnamon stick
3 tablespoons dark rum

To make the panna cotta

1. Put the cream, milk and sugar in a heavy-bottomed saucepan.

2. Cut the vanilla pod in half lengthways and scrape the seeds out. Add these to the pan, along with the pod. Bring to the boil, stirring occasionally.

3. Soak the gelatine in iced water for 5 minutes until soft. Remove it from the water, and squeeze it firmly to discard as much water as possible. Add it to the cream mixture, along with the rum, and stir until completely dissolved.

4. Pour the mixture into a jug and stand it in a bowl of iced water. Stir frequently until it starts to thicken.

5. Pour into ramekin dishes and chill in the fridge for 3-4 hours.

To make the spiced plums

1. Pre-heat the oven to 180°C/gas mark 4.

2. Spread a large sheet of tin foil on a work surface, and lay a square of baking parchment on top. Place the plums on the parchment, cut side up, and sprinkle with the brown sugar and diced butter. Add the star anise and cinnamon, and then sprinkle with the rum.

3. Gather the sides of the tin foil and scrunch together into a sealed parcel. Place this on a baking tray and bake for 20 minutes, then set aside to cool.

To serve

1. Run the tip of a sharp knife around the top edge of each panna cotta before dipping the ramekin into a bowl of very hot water for a few seconds.

2. Shake each ramekin firmly in your hand to loosen, then tip it carefully onto a serving plate. Add the spiced plums and juices.

Seasonal sides

When the days become shorter and colder, it's good to have meals that are filling and comforting. So tasty vegetable and potato dishes are welcome accompaniments, and these recipes will ensure everyone's well fed.

Cauliflower Cheese

Cauliflower Cheese

Even those who aren't keen on vegetables can't resist the indulgence of cauliflower cheese. It's the perfect partner for all kinds of meat dishes – and lovely on its own as a light supper.

Serves 4 30 mins preparation, 30 mins cooking

Ingredients
1 cauliflower
500ml milk
35g unsalted butter
30g plain flour
1 teaspoon English mustard
250g medium Cheddar cheese, grated
Sea salt and milled black pepper

Ovenproof dish

1. Pre-heat the oven to 180°C/gas mark 4.

2. Remove and discard the outer green leaves from the cauliflower. Carefully cut the florets away from the stem.

3. Heat a large pan of salted water. When it's boiling, drop in the florets and cook for 10 minutes, then drain into a colander.

4. Heat the milk in a saucepan. In a second pan, melt the butter until it's foaming, then use a wooden spoon to mix in the flour and stir for 2 minutes to make the roux.

5. Slowly add the hot milk to the roux mix, one ladle at a time. Keep stirring, and make sure you have a smooth consistency between each addition.

6. Once you've mixed in all the milk, reduce the heat and cook the sauce for another 10 minutes, stirring occasionally.

7. Remove the sauce from the heat, then stir in the mustard and 200g of the cheese. Check the seasoning, adding salt and pepper if necessary.

8. Arrange the cauliflower florets in an ovenproof dish. Pour the cheese sauce over, and scatter with the remaining cheese. Bake in the oven for 30 minutes.

Thrice Cooked Chips

If you've ever wondered how to get really crispy chips that are soft in the middle, try this recipe. There's simply no better way to do them!

Serves 4 10 mins preparation, 45 mins cooking

Ingredients
Rapeseed oil – enough to half fill a large pan or fryer
800g Maris Piper potatoes, peeled
1 tablespoon fine sea salt

Large pan or fryer
Food thermometer

1. Heat the oil in a large pan or fryer to 130°C.

2. Cut the potatoes lengthways into chips, no thicker than 1.5cm. Place them in a large pan and cover with cold water. Add a good pinch of salt and bring to the boil. Simmer for 7 minutes, then drain into a colander and leave for 2 minutes to dry off.

3. When the oil has reached 130°C, add the chips in batches and cook for 15 minutes until tender. Then remove from the oil and keep to one side.

4. Increase the oil temperature to 190°C. Add the chips, again in batches, and cook for 3-5 minutes until golden and crisp.

5. Remove them from the fryer, shake dry, and tip onto a tray covered with kitchen paper. Transfer them to a warm serving bowl, sprinkle with salt, and serve immediately.

Thrice Cooked Chips

Roast Autumn Roots, Sage and Maple Glaze

Most root veg are slightly sweet, and maple syrup enhances this to make a really satisfying side dish – lovely with roast meat or casseroles.

Serves 4-6 20 mins preparation, 40 mins cooking

Ingredients
1 butternut squash
½ celeriac
2 parsnips
4 carrots
½ swede
4 tablespoons vegetable oil
Sea salt and milled black pepper
2 tablespoons maple syrup
20 fresh sage leaves

Roasting tin

1. Pre-heat the oven to 200°C/gas mark 6.

2. Peel all the vegetables and cut them into equally sized wedge shapes. Place them in a large roasting tin and sprinkle with vegetable oil, then toss to coat evenly.

3. Spread them out in the roasting tin, season with salt and pepper, and roast for 25-30 minutes, until tender.

4. Pour the maple syrup over the vegetables and scatter with the sage leaves. Then put back in the oven to caramelise for another 10 minutes.

Roast Autumn Roots, Sage and Maple Glaze

Silky Mashed Potatoes

Silky Mashed Potatoes

There are many different recipes for mash. This is the luxury version, with double cream, which gives you rich, smooth results every time.

Serves 4-6 10 mins preparation, 30 mins cooking

Ingredients
1kg floury potatoes, peeled
Sea salt and milled black pepper
50ml double cream
40g unsalted butter

Potato ricer or masher

1. Cut the potatoes into small, equally sized pieces, and place in a large saucepan. Cover with cold water and add a good pinch of salt. Bring to the boil, then reduce the heat to a simmer and cook for 25 minutes, until the potatoes are really tender.

2. Remove them from the heat, drain in a colander and leave to stand for 2-3 minutes.

3. In a small saucepan, heat the cream and butter, bringing them to the boil.

4. Push the potatoes through a potato ricer, and back into the warm pan. If you don't have a ricer, use a masher, and try to get your mash as smooth as possible.

5. Using a wooden spoon, beat the potatoes while slowly adding the butter and cream, until you have a silky smooth consistency. Adjust the seasoning if necessary, then it's ready to serve.

Bonfire and Halloween

When you're huddled around the bonfire, you can't beat the traditional
goodies – and I've included plenty here. We've also got homemade treats for
the kids' Halloween tricks, and a few indulgences for the grown-ups too.

Pumpkin Tart

Pumpkin Tart

Apart from making Halloween lanterns, we don't use pumpkin enough. It's a really versatile ingredient – and this recipe shows how it lends itself to sweet dishes as well as savoury.

Serves 6 40 mins preparation, 2 hours 20 mins cooking, 1 hour chilling

Ingredients
300g pumpkin, peeled and cut into wedges
20g unsalted butter
150ml double cream
100ml full fat milk
½ teaspoon ground cinnamon
75g caster sugar
150g egg yolks (approx 6 egg yolks)
½ teaspoon ground nutmeg

For the pastry
230g plain flour
150g chilled unsalted butter, diced
1 pinch salt
75g caster sugar
Zest of 1 lemon, finely grated
2 medium eggs
1 medium egg yolk

18cm x 3.5cm flan ring
Baking beans
Roasting tin
Food processor

To make the pastry

1. In a large bowl, mix the plain flour and butter using your fingertips, until it resembles breadcrumbs. Stir in a pinch of salt, the caster sugar and the lemon zest.

2. In a second bowl, beat one egg and egg yolk together. Add them slowly to the pastry, mixing to form a dough. Shape this into a ball, wrap it in cling film and chill in the fridge for 1 hour.

3. Pre-heat the oven to 180°C/gas mark 4.

4. On a floured surface, roll out the pastry until it's ½cm thick, then line the flan ring, letting it hang over the sides. Line the pastry with baking parchment and weigh down with baking beans.

5. Bake the pastry for 20 minutes, then remove the beans and parchment. Trim the edges and paint the pastry with the remaining beaten egg.

6. Place back in the oven for 7 minutes, then take it out and let it cool.

To make the filling and finish the tart

1. Place the pumpkin in a roasting tin, and smear with butter. Cover with tin foil and bake for 1 hour until it softens.

2. Purée the pumpkin in a food processor, then push it through a fine sieve and let it cool.

3. Turn the oven down to 120°C/gas mark ½.

4. Measure 200g of the pumpkin purée into a bowl, then whisk in the cream, milk, cinnamon, sugar and egg yolks. Pour this mixture into the pastry, almost to the brim, and sprinkle with nutmeg.

5. Bake in the oven for 55 minutes, then let it cool before slicing and serving.

Gingerbread

Gingerbread

This childhood favourite is actually quite a grown-up treat too – with the ginger and mixed spice. It's an easy recipe, so why not get the kids to help?

Makes 10-12 slices 20 mins preparation, 1 hour cooking

Ingredients
250g self-raising flour
½ teaspoon table salt
2 heaped teaspoons ground ginger
½ teaspoon mixed spice
1¾ teaspoons bicarbonate of soda
350g golden syrup
120g margarine
1 medium egg
275ml milk

Loaf tin, greased and lined

1. Pre-heat the oven to 140°C/gas mark 1.
2. Sift the flour, salt, ginger, mixed spice and bicarbonate of soda into a large bowl.
3. In a small pan, melt the golden syrup and margarine. Pour this mixture onto the dry ingredients, and beat together.
4. In a separate bowl, mix the egg and milk, then gradually add to the gingerbread mixture. Beat thoroughly and pour into the loaf tin.
5. Cook the gingerbread for 1 hour, then remove from the oven and let it rest for 20 minutes. Take it out of the loaf tin, and place on a wire rack to cool completely. Store in a cake tin for up to 3-4 days.

Bonfire Toffee

Bonfire Toffee

Dark, brittle and seriously sweet, this treacle toffee is great for sharing on Bonfire Night. It's a simple recipe, but make sure you use a sugar thermometer to help you get the temperature right.

20 mins preparation

Ingredients
900g soft brown sugar
300ml water
½ teaspoon cream of tartar
150g unsalted butter
250g black treacle
150g golden syrup

Sugar or food thermometer
18cm baking tray, lined

1. In a heavy saucepan, heat the sugar and water until the sugar has dissolved.

2. Add the remaining ingredients, stir once only and bring to the boil. While it's boiling, you may need to brush the insides of the pan with a pastry brush dipped in water – this prevents crystals from forming, which would ruin the toffee.

3. Using a sugar thermometer, test the temperature. The toffee should boil to 134°C, which is known as the 'soft crack' stage. Once you reach this, pour the toffee into the lined tray.

4. Allow it to cool completely at room temperature, then break it into small pieces and store in an airtight container for up to 1 week.

Toffee Apples

These are great fun for a Halloween or bonfire party. The crunch of the toffee is irresistible, with a lovely, buttery, homemade taste.

Makes 6 40 mins preparation

Ingredients
25g unsalted butter
250g caster sugar
2 tablespoons golden syrup
120ml cold water
Few drops red food colouring (optional)
6 small eating apples

Sugar or food thermometer
Skewers or lollipop sticks

1. Place the butter, sugar, syrup and cold water in a heavy-bottomed saucepan. Gently bring to the boil, stirring constantly, until the sugar has dissolved.

2. Simmer the mixture gently, without stirring, for 30 minutes, or until it reaches 138°C. You'll need to test this with your sugar thermometer.

3. Push a skewer or lollipop stick halfway into the top or bottom of each apple.

4. Line a baking sheet with baking parchment.

5. When the toffee mixture has reached 138°C, add the food colouring if you're using it. Then tilt the mixture to one side of the pan, and dip the apples in, one at a time, to coat them lightly. With each one, let any excess toffee drip back into the pan, and then stand the apple on the parchment. Repeat this with the other apples, and let them cool and harden before you eat them.

Toffee Apples

Toasted Homemade Marshmallows

Toasted Homemade Marshmallows

Makes 24 (approx) 40 mins preparation, 2 hours setting

Ingredients
450g caster sugar
170ml cold water
2 leaves gelatine
2 teaspoons vanilla extract
1 teaspoon vegetable oil
2 tablespoons icing sugar
2 tablespoons cornflour

To serve
Melted chocolate

Sugar or food thermometer
Electric mixer

1. Pour the sugar and 170ml cold water into a heavy-bottomed saucepan. Place it over a medium heat, and stir until the sugar has dissolved.

2. Reduce the heat and let the syrup simmer for 20 minutes, without stirring. Test the temperature with your sugar thermometer – it needs to reach 113°C.

3. Meanwhile, soak the gelatine in cold water for about 10 minutes.

4. As soon as the syrup reaches 113°C, pour the gelatine and water into an electric mixer and begin to whisk on a low setting. Carefully pour in the hot syrup, followed by the vanilla extract. Increase the mixer speed, and leave it to beat for 15-20 minutes, until the mixture is thick, cool and beginning to set.

5. Grease a baking tray with vegetable oil and line with baking parchment.

6. Mix the icing sugar and cornflour in a small bowl, then pour just enough through a sieve to dust the baking tray. Keep the rest for later.

7. Pour the marshmallow mix into the dusted tray, and use a pallet knife dipped in boiling water to spread it evenly and smooth the surface. Dust with a bit more (but not all) of the icing sugar and cornflour.

8. Cover it with cling film and leave to set in a cool, dry place – but not in the fridge. It will need around 2 hours.

9. When it's set, dust a clean work surface with the remaining icing sugar and cornflour. Turn out the marshmallow slab, cut it into even squares and dust with the remaining icing sugar and cornflour. Keep in an airtight container for up to 3 days.

To toast the marshmallows

Place them on a long skewer, and carefully toast them near an open fire. Or you could dip them into melted chocolate.

Damson Gin

Sipping homemade damson gin is a delicious way to keep out the cold. It's also very enjoyable to make – and extremely rewarding when it's fully matured.

Makes 3 x 500ml bottles 14 weeks steeping

Ingredients
350g fresh damsons
2 x 70cl bottles gin
350g caster sugar

3 x 500ml bottles
Airtight jars
Sieve and muslin cloth
Carboy bottles

1. Wash and dry the damsons carefully, then prick them all over using a fork (use a silver fork if you have one).

2. Place the damsons and the gin in an airtight jar. Seal it with the cork, and shake every day for 4 weeks.

3. Strain the gin through a muslin cloth, leaving behind the remains of the damsons. Add the sugar to the gin and pour it into the carboy bottles.

4. Shake the carboy bottles every day until the sugar has fully dissolved, for about 14 days.

5. Strain the gin again through a muslin cloth, and then bottle it.

6. Store in a cool dark place for 8 weeks before drinking.

Damson Gin

Hot Chocolate

Hot Chocolate

Bringing a touch of luxury to ordinary drinking chocolate is easy – simply add more chocolate! Plus a little cream...

Serves 2 10 mins preparation

Ingredients
400ml full fat milk
60g good quality chocolate, broken into small pieces
4 heaped teaspoons drinking chocolate
250g aerosol can of UHT cream
20g chocolate, grated

1. Pour the milk into a small saucepan, bring to the boil, then reduce the heat to a simmer.

2. Add the chocolate pieces, and stir until they have melted completely.

3. Place 2 heaped teaspoons of drinking chocolate in each mug. Then, using a teaspoon, stir as you pour in the hot, chocolatey milk.

4. Finally, squirt the cream over the top and sprinkle with the grated chocolate.

Lamona Appliance, Sink and Tap Collection

The Lamona range is exclusive to Howdens Joinery and has been selected to perfectly complement our range of kitchens.

Lamona appliances are designed to look great and are manufactured to the highest standards to ensure they are durable and reliable, use less energy and water, and run quietly, whilst providing excellent value for money.

You can choose from ovens, microwave ovens, hobs, extractors, fridges, freezers, dishwashers, washing machines, tumble dryers, sinks and taps, which are all designed to fit beautifully in your Howdens kitchen.

All Lamona appliances come with a 2 year manufacturer's guarantee and what we believe is the best after sales service in the UK.

You will have the reassurance that we supply 500,000 appliances and 600,000 sinks and taps each year to UK homes.

Lamona is available from stock in over 510 local depots to your trade professional. To find out more and for detailed product specifications, please refer to **www.lamona.co.uk**

The General Tarleton

An old coaching inn with contemporary comforts, The General Tarleton Inn is in the pretty village of Ferrensby close to both York and Harrogate. Owned and run by John and Claire Topham for the past 12 years, The General Tarleton is constantly evolving but always sticks to the basic philosophy of offering great service and excellent food and drink in a relaxed atmosphere, and if you are staying the night, a comfortable room to rest your head.

The focus is on food

In The General Tarleton kitchen, John heads an experienced and dedicated team. Menus change daily to reflect the seasons and the pick of the catch or crop that day. John gets a call most days from the fishing boats as they return to port and within hours the fish is in the kitchen. Yorkshire has an abundance of excellent suppliers which The General Tarleton has worked with over the years to obtain the very best seasonal produce.

The
General
Tarleton

The General Tarleton Inn, Boroughbridge Road, Ferrensby, Knaresborough, HG5 0PZ
Tel 01423 340284 www.generaltarleton.co.uk